EDGE BOOKS

Epic Disasters

# THE WORST VOLCANIC ERUPTIONS OF ALL TIME

by Suzanne Garbe

Consultant:
Susan L. Cutter, PhD
Director
Hazards and Vulnerability Research Institute
University of South Carolina

CAPSTONE PRESS
a capstone imprint

Edge Books are published by Capstone Press,
1710 Roe Crest Drive, North Mankato, Minnesota 56003.
www.capstonepub.com

Books published by Capstone Press are manufactured with paper
containing at least 10 percent post-consumer waste.

*Library of Congress Cataloging-in-Publication Data*
Garbe, Suzanne.
  The worst volcanic eruptions of all time / by Suzanne Garbe.
    p. cm.—(Edge books. Epic disasters)
  Includes bibliographical references and index.
  Summary: "Describes the worst volcanoes in history, as well as formation, types,
and disaster tips"—Provided by publisher.
  ISBN 978-1-4296-7658-8 (library binding)
  ISBN 978-1-4296-8016-5 (paperback)
  1. Volcanoes—Juvenile literature.  I. Title. II. Series.
  QE521.3.G37 2012
  363.34'95—dc23                    2011037485

**Editorial Credits**
Anthony Wacholtz, editor; Veronica Correia, designer; Marcie Spence,
    media researcher; Laura Manthe, production specialist

**Photo Credits**
Alamy: Christopher Pillitz, 14, Melvyn Longhurst, 11, North Wind Picture
Archives, 21; Capstone: 25 (top); Corbis: 6, 9, Axel M. Cipollini, 28, Roger
Ressmeyer, 22; Getty Images: Adam Majendle/Bloomberg, 18; NASA: 27;
Shutterstock: adam.golabek, map, Ami Parikh, 25 (bottom), beboy, cover (front),
bierchen, 4–5, Dr. Morley Read, 13, Sharn Cheng, 17, Wajtek Jarco, cover
(back), design element

Printed in the United States of America in Stevens Point, Wisconsin.
092013    007758R

# TABLE OF CONTENTS

# ERUPTION!

Right now, somewhere in the world, a volcano is erupting. In fact, there are most likely 20 volcanoes erupting as you read this!

A volcano is a vent in Earth's surface that lets **magma** and hot gas escape. Once the magma reaches the surface, it is called **lava**.

Volcanoes come in different shapes and sizes. They exist on land and underwater. Some eruptions kill thousands of people, while others kill no one. Eruptions can last one day or hundreds of years.

The strength of an eruption is measured by the Volcanic Explosivity Index (VEI). Ratings are based on the size and force of the eruption. The weakest eruptions are given a value of 0. The strongest eruptions in history have been given a rating of 8. However, a volcano doesn't have to rate high on the VEI to have a powerful impact on human life.

**magma**—melted rock that is found underneath the earth
**lava**—the hot, liquid rock that pours out of a volcano when it erupts

# BASIC TYPES OF VOLCANOES

A SHIELD VOLCANO is shaped like a warrior's shield. It is much wider than it is tall. It is formed by hardened lava flows.

A CINDER CONE VOLCANO has gently sloping peaks formed by fallen ash from previous eruptions. Most cinder cone volcanoes are shorter than 1,000 feet (305 meters).

A LAVA DOME is formed by lava that is too thick to flow. Domes grow from the inside, often in the craters or on the sides of larger composite volcanoes.

A COMPOSITE VOLCANO has steep sides formed by layers of ash and lava. It looks like a mountain and can reach up to 8,000 feet (2,438 m) high. These volcanoes are also called stratovolcanoes.

## FACT:

A caldera is a large, bowl-shaped crater at the top of a volcano. A caldera forms after an eruption causes a volcano to collapse. Many calderas are filled with water and look like lakes.

# THE DEATH CLOUD

MAJOR ERUPTION DATE: 1902

LOCATION: Martinique, an island in the Caribbean Sea

TYPE: lava dome

VEI: 4

People from the island city of St. Pierre on Martinique thought they had little to fear from Mount Pelée. They had lived in its shadow for more than 200 years without a problem. Then one evening in 1902, Mount Pelée erupted with a powerful force. In the morning, a super-hot cloud of ash and rock formed in the sky. Part of the cloud separated and sped down the volcano at about 100 miles (161 kilometers) per hour. It became known as a "death cloud." As it moved to the sea, the cloud lit ships on fire.

St. Pierre stood in the cloud's path. The cloud was strong enough to pull down heavy statues. A blanket of burning ash settled on the ground as it passed.

The eruption of Mount Pelée was the deadliest of the century. Experts think 28,000 to 36,000 people died.

The death cloud eruption helped start the modern science of **volcanology**. Scientists hoped to save lives by learning more about volcanoes and predicting their behavior.

volcanology—the study of volcanoes

FACT:

The "death cloud" in the Mount Pelée eruption is also called a pyroclastic flow. A pyroclastic flow is a dense, extremely hot cloud of gas, steam, ash, and rock.

# AN EXPENSIVE ERUPTION

MAJOR ERUPTION DATE: May 1980
LOCATION: Washington State, United States
TYPE: composite    VEI: 5

It was March 1980. After 123 years of silence, Mount Saint Helens began to stir. Thousands of small earthquakes rocked the volcano. One side began to swell up. Finally, on May 18, a strong eruption caused ash, rock, and gas to spew sideways from the mountain. The ash, rock, and gas traveled at speeds of at least 300 miles (483 km) per hour. An enormous cloud about 15 miles (24 km) tall spread out above the volcano. Pieces of ash in the cloud rubbed against one another, creating electrical charges. The charges formed flashes of lightning that sparked forest fires. Two inches (5 centimeters) of ash covered a nearby town. More than 200 homes and 185 miles (298 km) of roads were destroyed.

**FACT:**
During the 1980 eruption, the peak of Mount Saint Helens blew off. Afterward, the mountain was 1,313 feet (400 m) shorter.

The Mount Saint Helens eruption was very powerful, but only 57 people died. Few people lived near the volcano. Also, **volcanologists** predicted Mount Saint Helens would experience volcanic activity. Because of the advance warning, most people left before the eruption.

Mount Saint Helens is the most expensive volcanic eruption in U.S. history. The eruption caused $1 billion in damages to the surrounding area.

volcanologist—a person who studies volcanoes

MAJOR ERUPTION DATE: AD 79
LOCATION: Pompeii and Herculaneum near the Bay of Naples, Italy
TYPE: composite    VEI: 5

Almost 2,000 years ago, Pompeii and Herculaneum were two successful cities in Italy. They were at the foot of Vesuvius, a large mountain. The soil was good for farming, and the mountain seemed peaceful.

An earthquake hit the two cities in the first century. Over time more earthquakes rocked the ground. Today's scientists know that earthquakes often come before volcanic eruptions. However, it's likely that no one living at that time knew that Vesuvius would erupt. Gas and ash spewed from the volcano. The wind carried some of the gas and ash to Pompeii, and ash rained from the sky. The ash blocked out the sun, creating total darkness.

The worst was still to come. Burning flows of hot ash and gas rolled out of the volcano. Pompeii and Herculaneum were completely destroyed. Herculaneum was buried by about 75 feet (23 m) of volcanic debris. An estimated 25,000 people died. The shapes of people who died were preserved underground beneath thick layers of ash.

# ERUPTION OF VESUVIUS

The eruption of Vesuvius is the oldest volcanic eruption with a written eyewitness account. This comes from a man named Pliny the Younger, who watched the eruption from a nearby town. He wrote:

"A dense black cloud was coming up behind us, spreading over the earth like a flood ... ashes began to fall again, this time in heavy showers. We rose from time to time and shook them off, otherwise we should have been buried and crushed beneath their weight ... At last the darkness thinned and dispersed ... We were terrified to see everything changed, buried deep in ashes like snowdrifts."

People poured plaster into the holes left in the ash. The plaster casts showed the outlines of human bodies.

**FACT:**

When ash and lava mix with dirt, the soil becomes rich and good for farming. As a result, people throughout history have often lived near volcanoes.

# A PREVENTABLE TRAGEDY

MAJOR ERUPTION DATE: November 1985
LOCATION: Armero, Colombia
TYPE: composite    VEI: 3

The Nevado del Ruiz eruption in 1985 pitted hot against cold. At its **summit,** Nevado del Ruiz was covered with snow and ice. But the frozen peak quickly disappeared with an eruption on November 13. The summit melted and created deep flows of muddy debris called **lahars.** The lahars swept down the volcano and rushed across the land.

Just before midnight, mud and debris rushed into the nearby town of Armero. More than 20,000 people were killed. A Colombian geology student described the event. "There was total darkness, the only light was provided by cars … We were running and were about to reach the corner when a river of water came down the streets. Looking towards the rear of the hotel I saw something like foam, coming down out of the darkness … It was a wall of mud approaching the hotel."

Volcanologists had warned about a possible disaster. They said an eruption and mudflows from Nevado del Ruiz was likely. Earthquakes had shaken the area for years. But the leaders of Armero weren't convinced. They didn't want to evacuate the town unless an eruption would definitely occur. The lack of an official warning system and emergency response made Nevado del Ruiz a very deadly eruption.

summit—the peak of a mountain
lahar—a volcanic mudflow

# MORE THAN A VOLCANO

MAJOR ERUPTION DATE: June 1991

LOCATION: Philippine Islands

TYPE: composite   VEI: 6

Before Mount Pinatubo erupted, it had been **dormant** for about 600 years. Then from March to June in 1991, thousands of small earthquakes hit the area. Steam and gas slowly erupted from the volcano. Then one day in the middle of June, gas and ash formed a mushroom cloud as wide as the state of California. The cloud was so big it blocked out the sun.

The same day, **Typhoon** Yunya arrived with heavy rain and strong winds. The ash turned into a substance like wet concrete. The heavy material caused roofs to collapse. Rivers running down the volcano became lahars that surged across the land. Piles of debris left behind were as deep as 650 feet (198 m).

Despite the destruction, only 300 people died. Scientists and local officials had learned a lesson from the eruption of Nevado del Ruiz. They moved more than 75,000 people to safety before the eruption.

FACT:
Mount Pinatubo is part of a large chain of volcanoes around the Pacific Ocean. This chain is known as the Ring of Fire.

dormant—describes a volcano that isn't active
typhoon—a hurricane that forms in the western Pacific Ocean region

# THE DECADES-LONG ERUPTION

**MAJOR ERUPTION DATE:**
1983-present
**LOCATION:**
Hawaii, United States
**TYPE:** shield    **VEI:** 1

Did you know that the entire state of Hawaii is made up of volcanoes? Five volcanoes form the Big Island of Hawaii. Of those five, Kilauea is the most active. The Kilauea eruption that began in 1983 registered only a 1 on the VEI. But Kilauea has been erupting ever since. The lava flows have covered more than 24,700 acres (10,000 hectares). Hundreds of people have been forced to leave their homes. Those that stay must be on the alert for volcanic activity. One resident said, "Even though we are used to the volcanic dangers and know how to respond, that doesn't make it easier."

**FACT:**
As of 2011, the United States is home to 169 active volcanoes.

Because Kilauea is easy to get to, scientists are able to study the island closely. Volcanologists can monitor the volcanic activity safely from different areas of the volcano, even the caldera. That's why Kilauea is one of the most studied volcanoes in the world. Because of its long-lasting eruption, it also may be the most active volcano on Earth.

# A YEAR WITHOUT A SUMMER

**MAJOR ERUPTION DATE:** 1815
**LOCATION:** Sumbawa Island, Indonesia
**TYPE:** composite
**VEI:** 7

the caldera of
Mount Tambora

The 1815 eruption of Mount Tambora started quietly. Between 1812 and 1815, Tambora released clouds of steam and caused minor earthquakes. April 1815 marked the end of the volcano's quiet rumblings. Several huge explosions blew the volcano's peak apart. One witness described "columns of flames" and rocks "as large as the head." Ash and **pumice** filled the sky and blocked out the sun.

The eruption was so strong that dust and ash circled the planet several times. As a result, less sunlight reached Earth. The average world temperature dropped several degrees. The eruption led to bad storms, flooding, and ruined crops, which caused **famine** and disease. Some regions even got frost and snow in the summer. That's why some people call 1816 "the year without a summer."

At least 80,000 people around the world died from starvation and disease. Scientists believe this is the highest death toll of any volcanic eruption.

**FACT:**
During the Tambora eruption, several famous writers were on vacation in Switzerland. The bad weather kept them inside, where they worked on writing stories. Mary Shelley wrote her famous novel *Frankenstein* during the stay.

pumice—a lightweight, gray volcanic rock
famine—a serious shortage of food resulting in widespread hunger and death

# THE LOUDEST SOUND IN HISTORY

MAJOR ERUPTION DATE: 1883
LOCATION: Indonesia
TYPE: composite   VEI: 6

In 1883 three mountain cones jutted up from the sea in Indonesia. The cones were the tips of a partly underwater volcano called Krakatau. In May 1883, one of the cones began to spew dust and ash. It didn't seem dangerous. Tourists came in boats to watch the activity. But they didn't realize the risk they were taking.

On August 26, 1883, Krakatau erupted in one of the biggest volcanic explosions ever recorded. The eruption was heard more than 3,000 miles (4,828 km) away. It has been called "the loudest sound in history." The resulting ash covered 300,000 square miles (777,000 square kilometers). In some places, the debris was up to 200 feet (61 m) deep. The eruption lasted two days and ended in a stunning moment—the volcano split apart. Most of it sank under the ocean.

No one lived on Krakatau, so few people died right away. However, when the volcano collapsed, it caused huge **tsunamis**. Some were 14 stories tall. The tsunamis slammed into Indonesia and other islands, killing more than 30,000 people.

tsunami—a large, destructive wave caused by an earthquake, volcanic eruption, or landslide

# A SCAR LEFT BEHIND

MAJOR ERUPTION DATE: 1792
LOCATION: Japan
TYPE: composite
VEI: 2

lava erupting from
Mount Unzen in 1991

In 1792 a volcanic eruption in Japan started a chain reaction of destruction. A lava dome erupted on the side of Mount Unzen. The eruption sparked a landslide. Mud and debris crashed through the city of Shimabara, Japan. The eruption also caused a tsunami in the Ariake Sea. The tsunami traveled 43 miles (69 km) along the coast. It wiped out almost 6,000 homes. More than 14,000 people died as a result of the eruption, landslide, and tsunami. This makes Unzen one of the most destructive volcanic eruptions in history.

In 1991, after almost 200 years of silence, Unzen erupted again. However, warning systems and **evacuation** plans saved thousands of lives. Forty-three people died in the 1991 eruption.

Unzen is still a threat to people in Japan. The path of the 1792 landslide appears as a scar—and a reminder—on the volcano's side today.

evacuation—leaving a dangerous place to go somewhere safer

# AN ANCIENT ERUPTION

MAJOR ERUPTION DATE:
about 640,000 years ago
LOCATION: Wyoming,
United States
TYPE: caldera VEI: 8

The ancient eruption of the Yellowstone Caldera is hard to imagine. Pyroclastic flows rushed through what is now Wyoming and nearby states. Volcanic ash fell across the land that today makes up the whole country. Some scientists think the Yellowstone eruption was 1,000 to 2,500 times stronger than the eruption of Mount Saint Helens.

Today the United States would have trouble surviving a similar eruption. Huge earthquakes would shatter windows 300 miles (483 km) away. Ash and debris would cloud the sky, causing total darkness for days. Pyroclastic flows would destroy farms and towns. The global temperature would drop.

Scientists estimate that the Yellowstone Caldera erupts every 600,000 to 800,000 years. Another explosion is possible in the near future. However, scientists don't think a major eruption will happen for several thousand years.

A similar eruption from the Yellowstone Caldera (red) today would be devastating. The affected area (brown) would include the western half of the country.

**FACT:**

The Yellowstone Caldera is located in what is now Yellowstone National Park. Some of the biggest attractions in the park are geysers, including the famous Old Faithful. The geysers are created when water mixes with magma underground.

geyser—a hot underground spring that shoots hot water and steam through the ground

# THE BIGGEST ERUPTION IN HISTORY

MAJOR ERUPTION DATE:
about 72,000 BC
LOCATION: Indonesia
TYPE: composite with lava domes
VEI: 8

Can you imagine living in darkness for days at a time? That's what happened during the Toba eruption, one of the most powerful volcanic eruptions in human history. Like Yellowstone, it had a VEI of 8. However, some scientists think the Toba eruption was twice as big as the Yellowstone eruption.

The Toba eruption had a big impact on the world. The hovering dust and ash caused the region to be completely dark for weeks. Six years passed before all the ash in the air settled to the ground. The eruption changed the weather, caused water shortages, and ruined crops. Half the trees in the northern part of the world died. Some scientists believe the Toba eruption caused the human race to shrink to about 15,000 people.

The Toba eruption was a powerful volcanic eruption. But scientists don't believe we will experience such an extreme eruption anytime soon.

An infrared image of Indonesia shows the lake that remains from the ancient volcano.

LAKE TOBA

FACT:
Both Toba and the Yellowstone Caldera are sometimes called supervolcanoes. A supervolcano can cause a VEI-8 eruption. This type of eruption can change the whole planet's weather.

supervolcano—a volcano that can erupt with a rating of 8 on the Volcanic Explosivity Index

# LIVING WITH VOLCANOES

Many people in the past were surprised by volcanic eruptions. But we aren't as likely to be surprised today. Scientists now have many tools to study volcanoes. They are able to predict when a volcano is likely to erupt. People often have more time to move to safe areas.

A volcanologist wearing fireproof clothing takes lava samples from an active volcano.

# If you live near an active volcano, here are some tips to help you stay safe:

- Find out how your local government has prepared for an eruption. Ask local officials how they will notify the community if the volcano becomes dangerous.

- Listen to the radio for emergency broadcasts.

- Have an emergency plan in case of an eruption. Your family should decide where to go if you are told to evacuate.

- Keep a supply of food and water on hand.

- Store dust masks and goggles to protect against falling ash. Be sure there are enough for each person in your family.

- Make a disaster kit that includes batteries, flashlights, blankets, and a first-aid kit.

The U.S. Geological Survey (USGS) studies volcanoes in the United States. USGS scientists take readings near volcanoes and measure the level of volcanic activity. If they think a volcano is becoming dangerous, they use an alert system to warn people. The USGS also has a team of scientists that responds to volcanic threats around the world.

# GLOSSARY

**dormant** (DOOR-munt)—describes a volcano that isn't active

**evacuation** (i-va-kyuh-AY-shun)—leaving a dangerous place to go somewhere safer

**famine** (FAM-in)—a serious shortage of food resulting in widespread hunger and death

**geyser** (guy-ZER)—a hot underground spring that shoots hot water and steam through the ground

**lahar** (LAH-har)—a volcanic mudflow

**lava** (LAH-vuh)—the hot, liquid rock that pours out of a volcano

**magma** (MAG-muh)—melted rock that is found underneath the earth; volcanoes spew magma out of the ground as lava

**pumice** (PUHM-iss)—a lightweight, gray volcanic rock

**summit** (SUHM-it)—the peak of a mountain

**supervolcano** (soo-per-vol-KAE-no)—a volcano that can erupt with a rating of 8 on the Volcanic Explosivity Index

**tsunami** (soo-NAH-mee)—a large, destructive wave caused by an ocean disturbance, such as an earthquake, volcanic eruption, or landslide

**typhoon** (tye-FOON)—a hurricane that forms in the western Pacific Ocean region

**volcanologist** (vol-kuh-NOL-uh-jist)—a person who studies volcanoes

**volcanology** (vol-kuh-NOL-uh-jee)—the study of volcanoes

# READ MORE

**Fradin, Judith Bloom.** *Volcano!: The Icelandic Eruption of 2010 and Other Hot, Smoky, Fierce, and Fiery Mountains.* National Geographic Kids. Washington, D.C.: National Geographic, 2010.

**Leavitt, Amie Jane.** *Anatomy of a Volcanic Eruption.* Disasters. Mankato, Minn.: Capstone Press, 2012.

**Lindeen, Mary.** *Anatomy of a Volcano.* Shockwave. New York: Children's Press, 2008.

**Person, Stephen.** *Devastated by a Volcano!* Disaster Survivors. New York: Bearport Pub., 2010.

# INTERNET SITES

FactHound offers a safe, fun way to find Internet sites related to this book. All of the sites on FactHound have been researched by our staff.

Here's all you do:

Visit *www.facthound.com*

Type in this code: 9781429676588

# INDEX